THE BOOK OF
BEST

OWEN O'REILLY lives in Dublin where he is a
third-level lecturer. He is author of the successful
The Little Book of Keane, 2002.

GW00692261

THE BOOK OF
BEST

Owen O'Reilly

The Collins Press

Published in 2006 by
The Collins Press
West Link Park
Doughcloyne
Wilton
Cork

British Library Cataloguing in Publication Data

O'Reilly, Owen
    The book of Best
    1. Best, George, 1946- – Anecdotes 2. Best, George, 1946—
    Quotations
    I. Title
    796.3'34'092

    ISBN-10: 1905172249
    ISBN-13: 978-1905172245

Typesetting: The Collins Press

Font: Palatino, 10 point

Printed in Malta

Cover images:
Front (centre): George Best, Manchester United, 1968, by PA, courtesy
PA/EMPICS;
(right): George Best playing for Manchester United against Benfica,
European Cup Final 1968, by Barratts, courtesy EMPICS/Alpha;
(left): George Best relaxing in his fashion boutique, by Peter Robinson,
courtesy EMPICS Sports Photo Agency

CONTENTS

Many thanks to Jonathan Williams

With love to Charlene and Isabel.
It makes all the difference in the world
to have you both with me

INTRODUCTION

This book is a collection of quotes by and about George Best. From Belfast to Manchester and on to the world, George's life was a rollercoaster that ultimately ended in a sea of tributes and an emotional funeral at home in Belfast.

Each chapter deals with some significant time of his life and features attributed quotes from commentators, colleagues, friends and foes. All other quotes are from George himself and help portray the essential character of the man and the times.

We could all have been 'someone' and, for many, being George Best would be the best of all. We wished upon the shooting star that was this intoxicating talent. Boys wanted to be him and girls wanted to be with him.

It was the swinging sixties and George was going to swing more than most. With Beatlemania at its height he became known as the fifth Beatle, and with his looks and impish character, Best became an icon. Above all, it was going to be the best of times with and for George Best, superstar.

As football's first celebrity, he enjoyed the high life. Compulsively competitive in conquering both opponents and beautiful women, he instinctively couldn't bear to be beaten. When the great Manchester United team prematurely went into decline, his frustration with the mediocrity led him to distraction.

Through the highs and the lows Best remained a fascination to the public and always deemed news-worthy. He lived under the constant gaze of public scrutiny. For the shy boy from Belfast with a weakness for alcohol, this proved quite a weight.

When all is said he will be remembered for his dazzling football. There has been no one like him since. He and the times were electric. He carried our hopes, dreams and desires on the field of dreams. He made football and life into theatre as we watched from the wings. He brought magic to the crowd and we loved him for it. He made us feel good and that was his greatness.

Being George

George Best's favourite television programmes were quizzes like 'Countdown' and 'Fifteen to One'. This scholarship student was the only one in his class to pass the eleven plus school exams. At his corner table at the Phene Arms, half-hidden but with an unobstructed view of the door, he enjoyed his *Daily Mirror* crossword. But behind all the headlines, what made George tick, what was it like being George?

'Not fancy you? Don't be ridiculous, George. Everybody fancies you.'
Germaine Greer, contemporary, social commentator

'I just remember having the best times that I've ever had in my life. To be with George was such fun you just can't put it into words.'
Malcolm Wagner, aka Waggy, former business partner and owner of the Village Barber, which was next door to Best's Manchester boutique Edwardia

'If I'd been born ugly, you'd never have heard of Pelé.'

'I was born with a great gift and sometimes with that comes a destructive streak. Just as I wanted to outdo everyone when I played, I had to outdo everyone when we were out on the town.'

'… like being a naughty boy wanting to prove how much I could get away with … I got away with more and more things. I pushed the stakes even higher.'

'If anyone said, "You don't need another drink, George", that would only make me want it even more. And if someone said of a girl I fancied, "Stay away from her, she's married", I would not rest until I had pulled her.'

'I wouldn't let anyone beat me if I had a glass in my hand … Drink is the only opponent I've been unable to beat.'

'There are people who still believe that I've never really grown up! Perhaps being forced to live in the spotlight from such a young age has made me more mature in some ways and less in others.'

'I'd always run away from trouble and I wasn't inclined to run towards it.'

'I didn't worry about things like bills and bank statements. I never have, and I couldn't tell you what is in my bank account at the moment.'

'I have always loved collecting … Be it wine, teddy bears, stamps, football cards, antique pens, or matchboxes. Unfortunately, my prized possession, the matchboxes, were slung by Alex [his second wife] in a fit of domesticated madness … It's a shame, as I picked the boxes up everywhere I went. You could probably have traced back journeys to all sorts of places I couldn't remember going to.'

'I'll cry all the way through sad films … We all like to think we're hard men but I'm a big softie, really.'

'Maybe "loner" is too strong a word but I've always enjoyed being on my own and that I could be on my own in a crowded room … perfectly happy.'

'I used to love going to Amsterdam, not because I wanted to pay for a woman or smoke dope, I just loved sitting in the old square having a couple of beers and watching the world go by.'

'I've always told every woman I've lived with, "Look, there are times when I just want to go off on my own for a few days", which I suppose is how everyone feels in a relationship.'

'I felt that her death [his mother's] was all my fault, that if I hadn't gone to England, hadn't done the things I'd done and if I'd only gone home more often … It's a terrible thing, guilt.'

'I might have been great at coping with pressure on the field but I've clearly never been able to handle it in normal life and I've never liked confrontation.'

'It is a funny feeling reading your own obituaries. But most of the writers were pretty kind and reports of my death gave me hours of entertainment.'
After he had been admitted to hospital in March 2000

'I was in for ten hours and had 40 pints – beating my previous record by twenty minutes.'
On his blood transfusion for his liver transplant

'All the bad times cannot wipe away the good memories, and despite all the ups and downs, when I look at my life as a whole, it is impossible for me not to feel blessed.'

'I feel I achieved everything I dreamed of as a child.'

'Que Sera.'
The name he gave to the house he had built in Manchester

'One of the few fellas I know who does *The Times* crossword.'
Paddy Crerand, former Manchester United team-mate

'Those who knew him testify to the essential kindness of his nature. This quality, combined with smouldering good looks and the most audacious presence on a soccer field that England had ever seen, made Best helpless against his own power and attractiveness.'
Keith Duggan, The Irish Times

'If people had come to him in those days, which they did on many occasions, and asked him to visit kids in hospital or visit a home, he'd have been the first one there.'
Pat Jennings, Northern Ireland goalkeeper, 1964-86

'Best always liked bars that functioned as a home for those who didn't belong anywhere else ... Bars where human vulnerability was not frowned upon, was, on the contrary, celebrated.'
Eamon Dunphy, Manchester United team-mate in the early 1960s

'I remember him [Busby] telling me a long time ago, when George was still very young, only in his early twenties and at the height of his fame, that he believed that one day he'd top himself. And all his life since then has been a suicide note, in a way.'
Michael Parkinson

BELFAST BOY

Born in Belfast on 22 May 1946, the son of a ship-yard worker, George Best grew up on Belfast's Cregagh estate and played football for both Cregagh Boys' Club and Lisnasharragh Intermediate School.

Best, the oldest of five children, was the only boy in his class to pass the eleven plus school examinations and he won a scholarship to the local grammar school, Grosvenor High. As a child he mastered kicking a tennis ball against doorknobs and even insisted on taking a ball to bed.

In 1961 it was a long, long way from Belfast to Manchester and after one day of his Manchester United trial he returned homesick to Belfast.

'We never had any problems finding him in the evenings, he'd still be there, banging the ball against the garage, after all the other kids had gone home.'
Dickie Best, Best's father

'I've lovely memories of home. Very, very happy … I had the happiest childhood of all time.'

'My first memory is kicking a ball around outside my grandmother's house when I was about twelve months old.'

'My other granddad, James "Scottie" Best, lived right beside the Glentoran football ground, The Oval. Now, growing up in those days, even football support was divided on sectarian grounds … If you were Protestant, you automatically supported Linfield and if you were a Catholic you supported Glentoran … Our family were Protestant, Free Presbyterians to be exact, but because Granddad Best lived next to the Glens' ground, I supported them.'

'I liked the singing and reading the Bible and, even now, I still pray at times.'
About going to Sunday School as a child

'Through the magic of television, I fell in love with another football team. Wolverhampton Wanderers.'

'I was mesmerised by those games [Wolverhampton Wanderers against European teams like Moscow Spartak]. The football was fantastic … But it was the floodlights that made them magical for me, made football into theatre.'

'Creed and colour have never been an issue for me.'

'To me they [his football boots] were absolutely beautiful … they were the best present I ever had and I would spend ages cleaning them and rubbing Dubbin into them to protect the leather before I played … Those boots were indestructible and, to prove it, I've still got them.'

About a Christmas present. Up until the age of thirteen or fourteen he had always played football in trainers because boots were 'far too expensive'

'… going on a boat to England was a big adventure and my Mum scraped together the money to buy me my first pair of long trousers for the journey in July 1961.'

About Best, aged fifteen, going for a trial with Manchester United

'I thought I'd never make the grade. It was my father who talked me into coming back.'

To Manchester United, aged fifteen, about running back homesick to Belfast after one day of his first football trial

'Manchester seemed such a big city and so different from Belfast but I wasn't going to go crawling back to Mum and Dad again and I decided that I would knuckle down whatever happened … I just didn't want Mum and Dad to think that I'd let them down again.'

'But gradually I drifted further and further from the family ... suddenly it was Belfast, not Manchester, which seemed like an alien world to me.'

'We are still a very close family.'

'He was everybody's hero, all the kids in the street wanted to be George Best. He could do anything with a ball, and he'll be sorely missed in Northern Ireland.'
Former Northern Ireland team-mate Gerry Armstrong

'George, you were an inspiration to a young man growing up in Northern Ireland. Kicking a football, a tennis ball or a tin can to and from school every day, pretending that I was scoring for United like you did so many glorious times. You will always be idolised by the red army. You stir a passion deep inside; a pride; a reason for living; a hope in dark times. It was a privilege to share the same world with you. Your legend will live forever. Your genius will never be equalled. You will always be loved.'
One of thousands of entries from a tribute website

'He never ever let us down [when they went over to UK over a twenty-year period]. He was always there – we went for meals with him and we just had such laughs with him. Just brilliant, brilliant times with him ... it was always just good fun.'
Barbara McNarry, Best's sister

FOOTBALLER

Left foot, right foot, head, dribble, balance, cross, tenacious tackling, speed, guts and courage; temperament for the big occasion; plus a large dash of genius and joy. It was a recipe for intoxication and the crowds loved him.

'The additional scope of George's achievement was how he made people feel when they watched him.'
Hugh McIlvanney, journalist

'I've always said that the best judges of a footballer are the players themselves and if you speak to anyone who trained or played alongside Bestie, they'll tell you the same thing. He took your breath away. The sad thing is that so little of what he did was caught on camera.'
Rodney Marsh, former footballer, Manchester City and Fulham

'People say he wasted his career. Nonsense. He was hunted down by defenders for eleven full seasons, starting at seventeen. He paid his dues all right.'
David Meek, veteran football correspondent of the Manchester Evening News, *1958-1995*

'Don't coach him – he's a genius.'
Matt Busby's advice to his staff after watching Best for the first time

'If he was to play on pitches like they do now, he'd be almost untouchable.'
Former Manchester United midfielder Ray Wilkins

Graham Williams, West Bromwich Albion full-back: Will you stand still for a minute so I can look at your face?
Best: Why?
Williams: Because all I've ever seen of you is your arse disappearing down the touchline.
Meeting, years after both players had retired

'The closest I got to him was when we shook hands at the end of the game.'
Northampton Town player Roy Fairfax, who had been marking Best when he scored six goals in an 8-2 FA Cup win for Manchester United in 1970

'Shellito was taken off suffering from twisted blood.'
United team-mate Pat Crerand after Best had given Chelsea full-back Ken Shellito a torrid time

'When the football was great and I was playing well, I couldn't wait to get up in the morning and that was the foundation of my life.'

'I loved training … and because I was physically strong for my size and had good balance, I rarely got injured or hurt.'

'I always felt like an entertainer out there and I knew I could get the crowd excited by doing things differently … to me it was pure theatre.'

'I worked harder on my left foot than my right and I became better on my left than my right.'

'I knew my weaknesses … It annoys me today when I see players earning £20,000 a week who can't kick with both feet.'

'I went to the gym every day and we used to have a ball strung up in there and if it was six feet off the ground I'd move it seven to try and reach it and spend hours trying to head it.'

'I used to dream about taking the ball round the keeper, stopping it on the line and then getting on my hands and knees and heading it into the net. When I scored against Benfica in the European Cup Final I nearly did it. I left the keeper for dead, but then I chickened out. I might have given the boss a heart attack.'

'I lived for playing … I never worried about the game, never thought about who we were playing and who might be marking me, I just went out and did it. Every game was like a new adventure, another dream.'

'I couldn't wait for the next game. I used to go into a bit of a depression after the final whistle went. It was either because if I hadn't played too well I wanted to carry on so I could play better and if I was having one of those games when everything was going right I wanted to carry on forever. So after the final whistle went, the first thing I thought about was the next game.'

'I set off. I beat one player, then another. By the end I had beaten five of them in the space of ten yards. I didn't know how I did it and still don't … When I see it on television, it still dazzles me.'
On what many consider to be his greatest goal, for San José Earthquakes against the Fort Lauderdale Strikers in 1981

'They'll forget all the rubbish when I've gone and they'll remember the football. If only one person thinks I'm the best player in the world, that's good enough for me.'

'This was always my beef against George as a player. If he got the ball he kept it. He made the other players look bad (whereas Beckham makes them look good) ... Everyone who discusses his brilliance as a footballer talks about his amazing ball skills, his courage, balance, grace, speed and dexterity, his way of slipping through the defence and leaving the keeper standing. No one talks about Best's team play. As far as I could see, there was little of that. If there was a game plan, Best would be sure to disrupt it.'
Germaine Greer

'He seemed to make the ball do what he wanted it to do. In all my experience in football I have never seen a player who could beat a man – or men – so close and in so many ways.'
Sir Matt Busby

'One of the greatest things he [Best] has is his temper; he has the temper for a big occasion.'
Sir Matt Busby

'The most naturally gifted player I have seen. He had the lot: balance, pace, two good feet, brave ...'
Johnny Giles, Leeds United contemporary

'There's been nothing like him since.'
Bobby Charlton

CLUB:
MANCHESTER UNITED

Manchester United scout Bob Bishop discovered Best playing for Cregagh Boys' Club. His legendary telegram to United read: 'I think I've found you a genius.' At fifteen Best joined United as an amateur and on his seventeenth birthday in 1963 he signed as a professional. Four months later, and weighing only eight stone, he made his league debut against West Bromwich Albion.

From 1967/68, he was United's top scorer for five consecutive seasons, averaging 25 goals a season. He scored his first League goal in his second match, against Burnley at Old Trafford.

Best's Manchester United pinnacle was achieved on 29 May 1968 when he scored in their 4-1 victory against Benfica in the final of the European Cup at Wembley Stadium. His final League match for United was a disappointing 0-3 defeat against Queen's Park Rangers on New Year's Day 1974.

'I wanted to sit him down and fill him full of meat and potatoes. He was so thin, so tiny. He looked more like an apprentice jockey than a footballer. I didn't give him a hope.'
Mary Fullaway, his landlady

'There are times when you want to wring his neck. He hangs on to the ball when players have found better positions. Then out of the blue he wins you the match, and you know you're in the presence of someone special.'
Paddy Crerand, Manchester United 1963-71, team-mate

'He was quite infuriating to play with.'
Denis Law, Manchester United team-mate, comments on Best's passing ability

'Well, you obviously weren't listening.'
Matt Busby greets Best at half-time of the European Cup quarter-final against Benfica, 1966. The Portuguese club had been unbeaten in nineteen European games at the Stadium of Light, and Eusebio had been presented with the European Player of the Year award before the kick off. Busby sent out his Manchester United team with the instruction to keep it tight for the first fifteen minutes, and then see what happened. Best scored two goals in the first twelve minutes!

'It was a very simple team talk. All I used to say was: whenever possible, give the ball to George.'
Sir Matt Busby

'The most fantastic thing about that first day as a first team player was walking down the tunnel and hearing the noise from over 50,000 fans … the hairs on the back of my neck really did stand up.'
14 September 1963, debut at home to West Bromwich Albion, aged seventeen. Manchester United win 1-0

'It proved … that I was able to stand up to the rigours of regular football at the highest level.'
On playing all but one of Manchester United's League games when they became champions in 1964/65 (41 games, ten goals)

'I didn't have any premonitions about how I was going to play – that's something you never knew – but I did know that I was ready. That, whatever the outcome of the game, this was the sort of stage I was meant to play on. The ground, the playing surface, everything was perfect.'
On playing Benfica in the Stadium of Light, Lisbon, in front of 75,000 fans in the European Cup quarter-final in 1966

'Well, perhaps on rare occasions I might have a lager. Then it gets back to the boss, Mr Busby, that you're drunk. I would like to have a flat of my own, but the boss thinks there might be temptation. Perhaps, when I'm 21. I've no complaints. I like my landlady … She's honestly like a second mother to me now. '
Aged nineteen

'He could be destroyed by a broken leg while playing on the wing for Manchester United today. Or he could destroy himself while still searching for something to replace the stern Presbyterian discipline which once packed him off to church thrice every Sunday. It is the second thought that disturbs him daily.'
Ian Wooldridge of the Daily Mail *in 1966*

'Wednesday till Saturday is murder. I know I've got to stay off the town and get to bed by eleven. But it drives me nuts. I don't read. Well, only the sports pages. The only thing that keeps me sane is remembering that there'll be a party on Sunday and Monday and Tuesday.'
1966 interview with Ian Wooldridge of the Daily Mail. *Best's fun-loving impulses were already being given worryingly free rein.*

'I'm sick of it. Right now I'd go anywhere I thought there could be success. I've got nothing against the management. It's the team. It's just not good enough. It's just not going anywhere. I could go right through the team and find things wrong. People knock me when I'm not doing it, but when I'm not doing it, who is? Brought along the right way, Sammy McIlroy could be a great player in five years. But I can't wait five years for Sammy to become a great player.'
February 1972

'It had nothing to do with women and booze, car crashes or court cases. It was purely football.

'Losing wasn't in my vocabulary. When the wonderful players I had been brought up with – Charlton, Law, Crerand, Stiles – went into decline, United made no real attempt to buy the best replacements. I was left struggling among fellas who should not have been allowed through the door. It sickened me that we ended up being just about the worst team in the First Division.'

On the disenchantment that led him to retire from Manchester United in 1972

'No one could ever have accused me of not doing it for United and if someone from the club had come and found me and spoken to me when I went missing, I would have listened … But no one ever did come.'

Best suggests that he could have been helped if the club had treated him more severely

'Once the crowd had gone, I went up into the stands and sat there on my own for almost an hour. I just sat and thought about all the good times I'd had and all the great occasions I've been involved in. The stands were empty and silent but in my head I could hear the roar of 50,000 people on that day when I first walked up the tunnel as a seventeen-year-old … lost in my own thoughts, all those great memories flooded into my mind and tears began streaming down my face.'

Realising his Manchester United career was over when he was not picked by Tommy Docherty, the manager, to play against Plymouth Argyle in the FA Cup, January 1974

COUNTRY: NORTHERN IRELAND

Best earned 37 caps and scored nine goals for Northern Ireland. Northern Ireland's manager Bertie Peacock, called up Best for his first cap in a 3-2 victory over Wales on 15 April 1964.

'It was just one of those nights that any parent would dream about for their son.'
Dickie Best, Best's father, on Northern Ireland's victory over Scotland, 1-0 at Windsor Park, 1967

'A master of control and manipulation who had ice in his veins, warmth in his heart and timing and balance in his feet.'
Danny Blanchflower, Northern Ireland captain, in 1970

'I was his room-mate. He played 37 times for Northern Ireland and I roomed with him on all those occasions ... He was not only a fantastic

player; to me he was also a fantastic bloke.'
Pat Jennings, Northern Ireland goalkeeper

'I just thought of the Irish trips as a bit of fun and once in a while get a few good results which we did.'

'When anyone asks me I say I'm Irish.'
As opposed to British or Northern Irish

'I've always said it should have been an all-Ireland team from the start. They do it in other sports so why not in football? I think the problem is it would do too many freeloaders out of a job from both sides. I think if you asked the players they would all agree that they would like an all-Ireland team.'

'Because, to be quite honest, the Republic of Ireland and Northern Ireland are never going to win a tournament; when they get together they have a chance.'
The primary importance for Best was having a chance of winning

'I had him when he was 21. He fascinated me. Even watching him in training – his movement, his skill, and he did it all so quickly. In that 1967 match against Scotland his virtuoso performance was the greatest I've ever watched – he controlled the game and had spectators rising from their seats every time he moved on to the ball.'
Billy Bingham, former Northern Ireland manager

EL BEATLE

When Best signed at seventeen as a pro for Manchester United in May 1963, it was two months after the release of the Beatles first LP, *Please Please Me:* 1964 and 'Beatlemania' was everywhere. The Beatles occupied several spots in the British Top Twenty and went on a US tour, appearing on 'The Ed Sullivan Show'. Pirate radio stations, operating from ships in the Irish Sea, were all the rage, with Radio Caroline being the most popular. Harold Wilson's Labour government took over at Westminster.

In the middle of this whirl was the beautiful Belfast boy with the appetite to go and a reputation enhanced by the novel sound of screaming adolescent girls wherever he played. He drove a series of E-type Jaguars, advertised every imaginable product and had to employ three full-time secretaries to field the 10,000 items of fan mail he received per week.

Oh yes he is (oh yes he is), oh yes he is (oh yes he is)
His world is built 'round discothèques and parties.
This pleasure-seeking individual always looks
    his best
'Cause he's a dedicated follower of fashion.
The Kinks were mates of Best and their big hit 'Dedicated Follower of Fashion' was supposedly written with Best in mind

'When he came on the scene he carried every young person's dreams in the sixties, it was a time of freedom of expression, an era that had come out of wartime, it was a liberation of young people in those days. And I think that George carried their dreams.'
Alex Ferguson

'The Return of El Beatle – Hat-trick at London Airport'
Newspaper headlines after the victory over Benfica in 1966. Best scored two goals in the game and the 'hat-trick' refers to the sombrero that he wore off the plane

'The first real footballing superstar and arguably the best player these isles have even seen.'
Former Liverpool and Republic of Ireland player, Mark Lawrenson

'Everyone, deep down, wanted to be George Best.'
Rodney Marsh

'I like to think of myself as a bit different from everybody else … I'm more like a pop star really.'
1965

'I was appearing more in pop magazines than football magazines.'

'I was probably the first footballer ever to have a pop star profile and my agent was right when he said we could put my name on stair rods and sell them to people in bungalows.'

'When I think back, they were probably the happiest days of my life, in 1966 and '67. Talk about fulfilling a dream – those days were just pure perfection, pure theatre … I was still only twenty … It felt like I was living in a fantasy world and could act accordingly.'

'I was the one who took football off the back pages and put it on to page one.'

'I went from El Beatle to El Vino in five or six short years.'

GAFFERS

'To be honest, I don't like him. He's too good-looking. It's competition for me.'
On José Mourinho, present Chelsea manager

'I think the great managers have to be ugly and swear a lot. Look at Alex Ferguson, Matt Busby or Brian Clough.'

'Sir Alex Ferguson's team is the best in the club's history.'

'It was tempting, particularly as it came from Big Ron, whose teams had always played football the right way, the way I liked to play, with formations based on attacking skills rather than defensive ones … [and he] didn't treat players like school kids, like some managers did.'
On Ron Atkinson asking Best to rejoin Manchester United in 1982 when Best was 36.

'The fact that I met Sir Matt makes it all worthwhile … A special special man … you can't really speak too highly of him because it is impossible.'
On Sir Matt Busby

'Sir Matt was very much the old school type, while I was the fifth Beatle.'

'Malcolm Allison [Manchester City manager in the late 1960s] was one of the game's most flamboyant characters ever. Famous for stormy relationships with bunny girls, fedora hats and large cigars that would make Monica Lewinsky wince, he loved his champagne.'

'All of his family [Sir Matt Busby's] one by one as we were leaving the graveside came up to me and said "You know he thought you were another one of his sons". It's a hell of a compliment coming from a man who was a great, great man. Not only a great manager but a great man. He had a special quality when he walked into a room: you knew you were in the presence of somebody a little bit special.'

'Besides Sir Matt only one other [manager] made an impact on me and that was Tommy Docherty. For me he was as bad as Matt [Busby] was good.'

'Tommy [Docherty] I have no time for at all.'

'The thing about George Best is that he could pass a ball beautifully but he couldn't pass a pub.'
Tommy Docherty

'George was gifted with more individual ability than I had ever seen in a player. When you remember great names like Matthews, Finney and Mannion, I can't think of one who took the ball so close to an opponent to beat him with it as Best did.'
Matt Busby, Manchester United Manager 1945-69, and 1970-71. He won the league in 1952/56/57/65/67, and the European Cup in 1968. He was knighted in 1968

'We had our problems with the wee fella, but I prefer to remember his genius.'
Sir Matt Busby, 1988

'It seems impossible to hurt him. All manner of men have tried to intimidate him. Best merely glides along, riding tackles and brushing giants aside like leaves.'
Joe Mercer, Manchester City manager, 1969

'Every manager goes through life looking for one great player, praying he'll find one. Just one. I was more lucky than most. I found two – Big Duncan and George. I suppose in their own ways, they both died, didn't they?'
Sir Matt Busby

PLAYERS

Some choice views on other players from Cantona to Beckham.

'How can someone who doesn't use his left foot, who doesn't know how to head the ball, doesn't tackle and doesn't score many goals be considered a great player. David Beckham is like the Kournikova of football.'

'I thought he was too good to be true. I was dying for him to say 'fuck' just once.'
Best of Bobby Charlton, the England World Cup hero and Manchester United team-mate.

'I'd give all the champagne I've ever drunk to have played alongside Eric Cantona in a big European match at Old Trafford.'

'If he thinks he's got pressure now, things are going to get ten times worse.'
On Wayne Rooney, 2004

'He's a special player – the most complete finisher I've seen in a long while. The way he puts the ball away reminds me of Jimmy Greaves at his very best – and Greavsie is my ultimate hero.'
On European Player of the Year 2001, Michael Owen

'Jimmy Greaves was undoubtedly the greatest goal scorer among my contemporaries at least and possibly the greatest ever in the domestic game.'

'Paddy Crerand was my minder on and off the pitch. As soon as I became known defenders came looking for me and he started looking out for them … And he was a fearsome prospect.
In 1972 Busby even got Best to move in with Crerand and his family in a bid to stabilise him

'Only for Leeds United did I wear shin pads. I knew I could avoid one, maybe two, hard players but not six or seven! They sent someone to watch me when I was fifteen … so I could have been a Leeds United player!'

'He's been very, very lucky – an average player who came into the game when it was short of personalities.'
On Kevin Keegan

'I once said Gazza's IQ was less than his shirt number and he asked me, "What's an IQ?"'
On Paul Gascoigne

'Roy [Keane] speaks his mind, which I love, but sometimes he does it too much. He needs to learn to keep his trap shut. He oversteps the mark … I hate to point out that when Man U did win the treble, Roy wasn't in the team.'

'Footballers today are millionaires by the time they're 22 or 23. More and more of them are going out and looking for something to give them a buzz outside football, be it gambling, drugs or booze. I got my buzz from playing. Players now have a groin injury for months and months and I often think they don't really give a toss whether they're playing or not because they're getting paid anyway.'

'I don't want to end up like him [Best].'
Paul Gascoigne, in 1990

'Keegan is not fit to lace Best's drinks.'
John Roberts, football writer, after Best said Kevin Keegan was not fit to lace his boots, 1982

THE HOLY GRAIL

To win the European Cup …

In 1968 United were beaten to the League title by local rivals Manchester City. But Manchester United went one better. This was finally to be their year. After all the emotion and tragedy of Munich, deliverance was to come in Wembley Stadium on 29 May. Manchester United won the European Cup 4-1 against Benfica. To many it seemed that Manchester United had fulfilled their destiny.

That year Best scored 32 goals in 52 games, including the decisive extra-time goal that made United champions of Europe. He was crowned English and European Footballer of the Year. He was still only 22 years of age. In the four seasons after the European triumph, Best missed just ten League games and scored 70 goals for Manchester United. It may have been United's Holy Grail but the stats show Best was keen for more success.

'They've done us proud. They came back with all their hearts to show everyone what Manchester United are made of. This is the most wonderful thing that has happened in my life and I am the proudest man in England tonight.'
Matt Busby after the match

'To this day I can still see Matt's face as the referee blew for time. It was a picture of elation but pain and relief as well.'
On winning the European Cup 4-1 against Benfica at Wembley Stadium, 1968

'We've achieved what we set out to achieve. It seemed they were all talking as if it was all over and I was only starting as far as I was concerned. And it seemed a little bit strange to me. I felt they should have been saying this was the first of many. Instead of this is the one.'
The attitude at Manchester United following the winning of the European Cup

'Alex, on balance, I have to say the late 1960s' side would win. Close match though. Maybe 1-0.'
Alex grinned and said with just a hint of sarcasm 'Only 1-0?'
'Well, one of us is dead and the rest are in their fifties and sixties.'
Best convinces Ferguson of the merits of the 1968 European Cup–winning team over the 1999 one

MISSING

Maybe it was his looks, humour, charm, lifestyle, money, cars, fame, athleticism, impish nature or twinkle in his eye. Maybe it was all these and more. Women found him an irresistible package and George was kind enough to be obliging.

'I've seen guys pull but no one like you [Best].'
Michael Parkinson

'I used to go missing a lot ... Miss Canada, Miss United Kingdom, Miss World.'

'Being a red-blooded male, the realisation at that time that I could have sex with almost whoever I wanted, whenever I wanted it, was a head-turning experience.'

'I was George Best and, mostly, I got my own way.'

'The gift of the gab helped … and I could lick my eyebrows.'
On why he was successful with women

'You might as well put your cards on the table. She can only say no.'
On turning up for a first date with Miss World with an overnight bag

'They say I slept with seven Miss Worlds. I didn't. It was only four. I didn't turn up for the other three.'

'Turning pro did mean a big increase in my salary and, to celebrate it, I treated myself to my first car – an Austin 1100.'

'I changed cars as often as most people change their shoes, buying a succession of Jaguar E-types.'

'A flash car gave you real pulling power in terms of the girls, not that I needed any help in that department.'

'I fell in love with a pair of knockers. It could happen to anyone.'
On his relationship with Eva Heraldsted, the striking Viking from Denmark, who sued Best for breach of promise to marry

'I later earned a reputation for dating two Miss Worlds ... But I went out with a lot of normal, working-class girls who were absolutely stunning – far more stunning than either of the beauty queens.'

'Pulling girls had become a sport for me and so I wanted to be the best at it.'

'I was still too young to think about settling down, especially with so many stunning and willing young women around ... I wanted to be able to come and go as I pleased.'

'Personally I had no interest in getting married, never gave it a second thought ... it was an era when you could do your own thing, and when we were on a night out, I always stayed longer than everybody else.'

'I bought a four-poster [bed] once and started making little notches and it collapsed after a week.'
On how many girlfriends he has had

'You only say you're in love, you've got to haven't you, but most of the time you don't mean it.'

'In 1969 I gave up women and alcohol and it was the worst twenty minutes of my life.'

'It was utter madness. Here I was, one of the world's most famous footballers and I had just decided not to play in an important game and instead went out on a date.'

The game: away to Chelsea 1971; the date: away with Irish actress Sinéad Cusack, Islington, London

'The craic at Ed's place was unbelievable. Talk about Bacchanalian. The scene was like the last days of the Roman Empire. There would be some of the most gorgeous creatures you'd ever seen sitting naked around the pool and talking to these famous actors as if the situation were perfectly natural. The champagne would be on tap and, apart from Bobby [McAlinden] and me, everybody would be smoking joints.'

While playing for the Los Angeles Aztecs in 1976, Best and McAlinden socialised with Ed Peters, who hosted parties at his Beverly Hills pad

'God, do you realise half the women in the world would pay good money to get that number?'

Reporter Sue Mott, taking Best's phone number

'Half the women in the world have got it.'

Best's reply

'I phoned my parents to tell them I'd got married, but I think they had already read about it in the newspapers ... they never criticised anything I did in my private life.'

GIRLS TALK

At sixteen Best fell for a girl from a local bakery while an apprentice at Manchester United. He notoriously claimed once to have bedded seven women during a 24-hour marathon romp in Manchester. His first beauty queen was Miss Great Britain, Carolyn Moore, in 1969, started his legendary seductions of some of the world's sexiest women,including Danish golden girl Eva Haraldsted, Joan Dekyuper, actresses Annette Andre, Susan George and Sinéad Cusack plus singer Lynsey de Paul.

By the time he sensationally quit top flight football in 1972, it was reported that he was drinking a dozen beers and several whiskies a day. Another Miss World fling followed in 1973 with American beauty Marjorie Wallace. But that relationship soon ended in a legal row over a fur coat. Then a three-year relationship with blonde model Angie Lynn wound up in a string of bust-ups.

In 1976 Best met *Playboy* bunny Angie MacDonald James and the couple wed two years later in Las Vegas. During this six-year marriage they had a son, Calum, born in 1981. The marriage finally ended when Angie discovered he was having an affair with the then Miss World, Mary Stavin. Following Mary Shatila, his lover of eight years, Best married in 1995 air hostess Alex Pursey. They divorced in 2004 because of Best's adultery and his conquests continued up to his death.

It is only fair to grant the right of reply to the women in Best's life.

'He's like a little boy. If anything doesn't go the way he wants, he'll stamp his feet and scream.'
Jennifer Lowe, ex-Miss England and former girlfriend, 1970

'Alex is a sweetheart but of course she is a nutcase to take George on. She is a very nice girl. She deserves a medal for marrying him. I just thank her every day for looking after him because he would have been dead years ago if Alex hadn't been around.'
Angie Best, former wife, on Best's second wife, Alex

'He seems to be on a mission to self-destruct and it's getting worse.'
Alex, his wife at the time, as he resumed drinking after his liver transplant, in 2003

'I remain good friends with George. He is the only man I ever loved.'
Angie Best

'George always got annoyed at celebrities who refused to talk to people in the street, or the pub. They bloody well put us here, he'd say; give something back. So he'd take a drink off them.'
Alex, by then his ex-wife, in 2005

Best: 'Why d'ye not fancy me?'
Greer: 'Not fancy you? Don't be ridiculous, George. Everybody fancies you.'
Best: 'So why not you?'
Greer: 'I do fancy you, George.'
Best: 'So why d'ye do nothing about it?'
Greer: 'Because I'm not a fool, George. Every time you come in here [Brown Bull pub] you've got a different blonde on your arm. Besides, there's someone in the team I fancy more.'
Best: 'Who? Who is it?''
Greer: 'Guess.'
Best: Alex Stepney? Tony Dunne? Billy Foulkes? Shay Brennan? Paddy Crerand? Bobby Charlton? Brian Kidd? John Aston? (George was stumped).
Greer: 'I'm not surprised you can't work it out. He's been playing opposite you and you haven't even seen him yet, let alone passed him the ball.'
Germaine Greer

'I knew nothing about alcoholics. I thought he was just one of the boys and needed, as all women do, to settle down to be mothered ... I'll change him. I had the Florence Nightingale syndrome going. But it was a mistake. Calum was a year old, I hadn't seen George for a week, and I was taking him [Calum] to the doctor for a check-up and I was driving down the street in San José. It's raining, it's a really dreary miserable day, and in the middle of the street ... this creature [is] walking towards me soaking, miserable, huddled over like a homeless person. And I realised it was my husband. And then I looked at my son and thought I can't do this any more and I realised that I couldn't look after two babies so the big one has to go ... But God bless George, he comes home to England, he is here for a week he meets Miss World [Sweden's Mary Stavin] and they fall madly in love ... Only George.'
Angie Best

'Alcoholism is a disease. It's not something he does to upset us all, it's not something he does on purpose to annoy the media or the world or his family or friends ... In his heart he is a child. He ends up feeling like a naughty boy all the time after anything he's ever done wrong.'
Mary Shatila, former girlfriend

'I don't know what that charm is – he's George ... I will always love him ... I do forgive him, as we all do, but I don't know why.'
Angie Best

FAME

Best likened his fame to living in a goldfish bowl in Trafalgar Square. It must have been a weird existence – every day dozens of people coming up to shake your hand and tell you that you were the greatest while paparazzi skulk around waiting for you to go into a bar or have an argument with your missus. Whispers of 'There's George Best' everywhere you go. Everyone with an opinion. 'Where did it all go wrong?' It's not that he didn't fan the flames himself with his lifestyle and his flamboyant touches like splashing out on a Rolls-Royce Silver Shadow on leaving United.

'When I first started playing I was the same as most kids. I'd like to see my name in the papers and read about myself no matter what it was, and I purposely used to do little things knowing that I'd get my name in the paper, but it really did sort of backfire; it became an ogre really.'

'I even found it difficult to watch myself playing on TV because I couldn't identify with the person on the screen … You feel like you are two different people and it's not a healthy experience.'

'It got so bad that I was afraid to go near the windows and I couldn't get away without a police escort. It was like being a prisoner.'

'Even at the height of my fame, 50 per cent of the people who saw me wanted a fight – it's the downside of being a star player.'

'I had become a superstar and it didn't feel anywhere near as good as I would have imagined.'

'It's hard work being a face or a name in England.'
1975

'There is always some lowlife who wants to impress his pals or a girlfriend and sets out to target you. He will get mouthy or start a punch-up and it gets thoroughly unpleasant.'

'All great athletes in our country [UK] are treated deplorably by the press – absolutely disgraceful. I think they believe they put you on that pedestal so they are entitled to knock you off whenever they want, which is a terrible way of thinking.'

DRINKING CANADA DRY

Apart from football and womanising, George Best was a world-class drinker. Perhaps it was inevitable living as he did under such a spotlight. His alcoholism led him to become a celebrated caricature drunk and led to his liver failure and death. At the end he allowed a ghastly deathbed photograph be published in the *News of the World* with the caption 'Don't Die Like Me', as a warning to others of the dangers of alcohol and alcoholism.

'I saw an advert on the side of a London bus inviting me to "Drink Canada Dry".'
On why he considered joining the Vancouver Whitecaps

'I never went out in the morning with the intention of getting drunk. It just happened.'

'Alcoholics will always take the line of expediency, telling loved ones what they want to hear.'

'When I finished playing, I tried to find something to replace that buzz. Maybe I thought drinking made me feel good.'

'I did most of my drinking on my own. Often I'd spend hours sitting in a corner. I'd drink and when I'd had enough I'd just get up and go home to bed.'

'I don't drink every day, but when I do it's usually for four or five days on the trot.'
1996

'I was becoming bored, so alcohol was relieving the boredom. I was looking for anything to fill the gap that football had left … For three years I was doing the same thing every night and every day … I was missing the one thing that had given me a high [when he retired] and I was looking for other things. The only thing I didn't try was drugs.'

'The gambling started to become a bit of a drug as well and I couldn't stop gambling and I didn't want to and I couldn't stop drinking and I didn't want to. The problem was I didn't have anyone to answer to.'

'I have had moments where things have seemed so bleak that I couldn't see any way out. The thought of never drinking again terrified me and I would have rather just given up trying to get better.'

'It became a vicious circle but I couldn't see that my drinking and my failure to turn up at training was a factor in the team's downward spiral. I probably felt that I could stop if I wanted to – and maybe I could have done if the team had improved. But I would have laughed if you'd said I had a drink problem.'

'I felt guilt over my Mum's death but like any alcoholic (which I was, though unaware of it) I didn't relate it to my own drinking. That may sound incredible but … I always – arrogantly – thought I could stop at any time.'

'Another time, I went almost a whole year without booze and then, with the logic only an alcoholic could understand, went out to celebrate and began another bender.'

'… only an alcoholic knows the real suffering that comes when the hangover is finished and the discomforts of the withdrawal kick in; the sweats, the palpitations and the panic.'

'I might go to Alcoholics Anonymous, but I think it would be difficult for me to remain anonymous.'

'It [alcohol] controlled me totally … I wasn't bothered whether I woke up in the morning or not and sometimes I wished I didn't … When your brain is that muddled and scrambled … especially if you don't know what you're doing with your life … it can be fairly depressing. The thing that kept me going was I kept thinking I'm going to miss too much.'

'The amateur psychologist liked to think you could point to an incident that triggers off a relapse but an alcoholic like myself doesn't need a reason … once it [alcohol] gets back into your system, God, it's lovely.'

'Today [1996] I don't have any problems. The alcohol is still there; it ain't going to go away, that's for sure … Today I find it difficult now to say I am an alcoholic because I don't drink every day and if I don't feel like a drink I don't drink and if I feel like a drink I do. But the big difference is very rarely today does it affect any other area of my life.'

'Unfortunately, there is no solution to alcohol.'

At Her Majesty's Pleasure

Best's fall from grace was compounded by his becoming an increasingly messy drunk. He publicly disgraced himself when he made a drunken appearance on BBC''s 'Wogan' in 1990. The switchboards were jammed after he swore repeatedly, including the immortal line, "Can I say shit?".

By this time he was a regular on the Chelsea pub circuit where he was involved in a fracas in the Wellington Arms. He was later convicted of assault and bound over by Marylebone magistrates court.

On 17 December 1984 Best's appeal against a three-month sentence, for drink driving and assault on a policeman, was dismissed and he was sent to Pentonville Prison. Ten days later he was transferred to Ford Open Prison in Sussex and later was released after eight weeks of a twelve-week sentence.

'After making one good decision to give myself up, I quickly reverted to making my most stupid one yet. I head-butted one of the policemen.'

Saturday 3 November 1984, after being caught drink driving, Best was released from Canon Row police station at 6am and charged to appear at Bow Street magistrates court at 9am. Being the worse for wear he, not unreasonably, went home to bed, assuming the court to be on the following Monday. With a warrant out for his arrest, there ensued a series of Keystone Cops situations which concluded with Best giving himself up. The police 'were obviously up for a fight after being messed about all day'.

'You little Irish wanker. You Irish scum. You little shit, you think you are a big star but you're just another piece of Irish dirt.'

What one policeman said on arresting Best.

'Not a pleasant experience.'

'I would lie on my bunk wondering what Dad and the family would be thinking and feeling frustrated that I couldn't even speak to them …'

'Between '63 and '73 ten years at the top … and here I was not so long afterwards, talk about rock bottom … So I had a long time to sit and look at myself and try and figure out what the hell was happening. That might have been part of the turn-around; maybe the start of it.'

'Well, I suppose that's the knighthood f***ed.'
While awaiting sentencing, at Southwark crown court, for drink-driving.

'I wouldn't recommend it [prison] to anyone.'

'Best hit rock bottom as the star of the team at Ford Open Prison.'
Economist

'It seems remarkable, given his career of drunk-driving, philandering and domestic violence, and his multiple addictions to alcohol, gambling and sex, that Best only went to prison once.'
Gordon Burn, The Guardian

REGRETS

In October 2003 George Best sold his 1968 European Footballer of the Year trophy at auction for £167,000. On the same day his 1968 British Footballer of the Year award failed to find a buyer. Even Best's European Cup winners medal is missing. Many people seemed to have regrets for George but he himself had too few to mention …

'I spent a lot of money on booze, birds and fast cars. The rest I squandered.'

'I took a penalty against Chelsea in 1971, and Peter Bonetti, the fucker, he saved it! I wish I'd sent it the other way.'
In response to the question, 'Is there one thing about your life you'd like to change?', Esquire magazine interview, 1991

'I'm not one to drive myself crazy by wishing I could turn the clock back.'

'Not at all. I regret nothing. I have a great lifestyle – and hope to continue to have one, after the [liver] operation …'
Asked if he regretted all the years of drinking

'I wouldn't change a single thing in my life. Women, alcohol, gambling … I would do exactly the same thing.'

'No, {regrets} because I've always made up my own mind. If you make up your own mind, you can only blame yourself.'

'My one big regret is that I didn't play on for ten more years.'
On retiring at 27

'I don't think that I ruined what you call talent at all. I played for twelve years with Manchester United and I won everything. I couldn't have done much more.

Maybe I could have played football at a certain level for a longer period, but I left for the United States, I stayed there for eight years and had a lot of fun there too. I did everything that I felt like doing. You know, my friend, mine was really a great life.'
Best to Italian magazine L'Espresso.

'Come on, let's get out and beat the rush.'
Best and his agent and best friend, Phil Hughes, left the 1999 European Cup Final with a minute to go. They missed the Manchester United goals from Teddy Sheringham and Ole Gunnar Solskjaer which beat Bayern Munich in Barcelona's Nou Camp Stadium

'If I was reincarnated, I'd like to come back as Bestie because he was a genius and had all them women and drank all that wine.'
Barry Fry, former Manchester United youth colleague of Best's, in 1998

'It's difficult to agree with the great plaudits for a man who had so many second chances and continued to abuse himself. It seemed that this was the way he wanted to go. In the end he seemed not too bothered and in some ways people in that position … are very selfish people and don't care about destroying themselves.'
Tony Cascarino, former Chelsea player and journalist with The Times, The Racing Post *and co-presenter of the early evening Talksport Radio show, Uk.*

'The only tragedy George Best has to confront is that he will never know how good he could have been.'
Michael Parkinson, broadcaster and personal friend

SALUTES AND HONOURS

Best received several salutes and honours including his Football League Championship winners medals, 1965 and 1967, UEFA European Cup winners medal, 1968, European Footballer of the Year, 1968, and Football Writers' Association Footballer of the Year, 1968. Honoured by the Football Writers' Association in 2000, in the following year he was named the top Manchester footballer of the past 50 years by a *Manchester Evening News* Sunday Pink Panel. In 2002 he was awarded a Lifetime Achievement Award at the BBC Sports Personality of the Year ceremony and he was presented with an Honorary Doctorate at Queen's University, Belfast in 2001 and was made a Freeman of Castlereagh in 2002.

'George Best.'
Pelé, in 1982, when asked who was the greatest player of all time.

'I was voted the 1968 English Footballer of the Year and European Footballer of the Year.'
Best was the youngest player ever to win the European honour at just 22

'Me and a mate picked up two darling birds and they took us back to their flat. I went into the bedroom with my bird and she started getting undressed. I was that drunk, I was standing there wondering how to get undressed without letting go of the award.

I went to sit on the bed, missed it by four feet and ended up lying on the floor. I remember the bird looking down at me, starkers, and saying, "Some player of the year". Then I fell asleep. I woke up still clutching my award and staggered out of the flat. I hadn't a bloody clue where I was.'
On the night he won the 1968 European Footballer of the Year Award

'It's a pleasure to be standing here. It's a pleasure to be standing up.'
On being made Footballer of the Century, 1999

'I couldn't believe it when they rang and told me. The only other person who has received the award is Sir Alex Ferguson ... A Beeb bod said to me, "You have been awarded the prize because you are, in many people's eyes, the greatest British footballer of all time, and a man who changed the perception of football in this country with your unique combination of skill and style." What can I say? That person is incredibly insightful – I hope they get a pay rise soon!'

On receiving BBC Lifetime Achievement Award at the Sports Personality of the Year ceremony. December 2002

'I recall once being in the jacuzzi with my old club Nancy [in France] with four French players and talking about the best player ever.
I mentioned George as you do, and none of them – four pros – had heard of him. I said: "The tricky winger, Man Utd," but they'd no idea.

It's perhaps a sign that he's more of a myth in Britain and Ireland. I think it might be quite naive to think he's known and adored all over the world. You'd be amazed how many people don't know him.'

Tony Cascarino

'Do you think if I played for Brazil and Pelé played for Northern Ireland, you'd still be saying the same thing?' [that Best was the world's second-best footballer]

Best's reply to his friend, the journalist Brian Medley

'Pelé called me the greatest footballer in the world. That is the ultimate salute to my life.'

FAREWELL OUR FRIEND,
BUT NOT GOODBYE

Like many shooting stars, George Best crashed and burned prematurely. He was buried on a dismal December morning in 2005. Over 100,000 people from all walks and parts came to stand and honour the funeral cortege. They loved him and they wanted to pay their respects and thank him for being who he was, which, perhaps, was all they wanted him to be.

'They were the best of times and the worst of times. You know, that perhaps aptly describes so many of our lives and it certainly was no different as regards George. I often think perhaps that those who criticised him with his illness would perhaps, rather than criticise, be better saying "there go I, but for the grace of God".'

Pastor Roy Gordon, who presided over the funeral, where this was said

'George Best was one of the greatest footballers of all time. Naturally athletic, tough, confident and blessed with genius, his career was one of the brightest stars of his generation. His gifts were legendary.

For the goals, the audacious dribbles and all the wonderful memories, Manchester United and its legions of fans worldwide will always be grateful.

We feel a deep sense of loss but his spirit and his talent will live on forever.'

Manchester United official club statement on Best's death, 25 November 2005

'The thing I remember, apart from his talent, was his courage. I can see him flying down the wing, riding tackles from people like Ron Harris, Tommy Smith and Norman Hunter. They were serious guys – you didn't mess with them – and it was when you needed to be struck down by a tomahawk just to get booked – yet he rode all that. Every time he went down, he got up again and just said, "Give me the ball". That will stick in my mind forever.'

Alex Ferguson, Manchester United manager at the time of Best's death

'It was often said that Bestie never gave Bobby [Charlton] or myself the ball, he never passed to us. It wasn't until last week when I was talking to Dickie [Best] that I actually found out why. He told us George said to him: "The reason I didn't pass to Bobby and Denis was they were always offside."'

Denis Law, commenting on the death of Best, his long-time friend and colleague

'Not only have I lost my dad, but we have all lost a wonderful man.'
Calum Best, at George Best's funeral

'What mere mortal could do what he did on a pitch? Today we celebrate his life.

In a country that often cannot rise above religion and politics, George Best did more than most to bring us together as people to make us recognise that maybe there is more that unites us than divides us. He belonged to us all and today, more than ever, we want to show the world how delighted we are that he came from a country of just one-and-a-half million people and became the best footballer the world has ever seen. George, we mourn your life cut short, but we are proud to welcome you home.'
Eamon Holmes, broadcaster, the funeral's master of ceremonies

'Today the world is saying goodbye to Dr George Best, superstar, superhero.

Today I am saying goodbye to GB, super brother, my hero. My love and respect for you, GB, was unconditional and simple. I will always cherish the memories of the many happy times that I was privileged to share with you.'
Best's sister Barbara McNarry

'I think, to be successful and to do something good you have got to be a fighter, and that is what he had.'
Denis Law, Manchester United colleague and life-long friend

'I was overcome with sadness at the death of George Best. He was the pin-up boy of my generation, the football genius, the "bit of a lad we all wanted to be". He played as we would have liked to have played, if we had been given the talent and the chance. He lived out our fantasies, in more ways than one.

His football was off-the-cuff, skilful, daring, imaginative and never nasty. He played to win, jinked and dribbled away from mesmerised opponents and scored fantastic goals … Goodbye George, we weep to see you go.

We are also crying for ourselves and our ideals, our dreams, our fantasies, our might-have-beens.'
Michael Power, letter to The Irish Times, *November 2005*

'I'll not get that call next May, sadly. But I've got my memories, they're all great; they're all good memories and nobody had a friend as good as George Best to me. And I'll never forget him, like everybody else.'
Bobby McAlinden shared the same birthday as Best, 22 May 1946.

TRIBUTES

The impromptu shrines of flowers, football scarves and jerseys laid as tribute to the memory of a fallen hero and the thousand magic moments he had created; ordinary people going out of their way to express their love and respect. Newspapers and television carried the tributes of the famous. Numerous websites carried the tributes and memories of the crowd. All were united in their desire to pay respect to the memory of George Best.

'He was a fantastic player. Everybody at United regarded George as being one of the greatest of all time. It's very sad because he was a wonderful person, who was very likeable.'
Current Manchester United manager, Sir Alex Ferguson

'He was able to use either foot – sometimes he seemed to have six.'
Sir Matt Busby

'He was on a par, at least, with anyone you can name. We at Manchester United have learned from our experience with Eric Cantona; we had to treat him differently, make allowances. If, instead of being hostile to George, which I was, we had leaned a bit his way and tried to help him, who knows?'
Sir Bobby Charlton

'From 1964 to 1969 he was the best player in the country. It's sad as hell but I don't think we saw the best of him. He went on the blink at a time when he could have got even better. He was not only a fantastic player; to me he was also a fantastic bloke.'
Denis Law

'The world of football has lost a great. Personally, I've lost a great old friend. I feel sorry for his family. At a moment like this we can remember how important this man was for the British and world football. He was fabulous.'
Eusebio, Benfica and Portugal football contemporary

'You could have put George in just about any position in our 1968 team and he would have been better than the person who was playing there.'
Manchester United European Cup-winning team-mate, David Sadler

'He was a complete player. There's not many of them about in the world or ever has been. He was

a fantastic man. He was very kind, very generous. There was no big-headedness about him.'
Former team-mate, Sammy McIlroy

'When you speak to people in Manchester, when they talk of the great players – and in my era it was Beckenbauer, Pelé, Cruyff – then George Best always seems to come into the equation.'
Birmingham manager, Steve Bruce

'The images of George in hospital were really upsetting, but I'd like to keep the image of him in the red shirt of Manchester United.'
Blackburn manager, Mark Hughes

'I remember my first pair of boots when I was four years of age was a George Best pair of boots. I used to go out and play with the locals and think I was George Best, trying to take on everyone, beat everyone.'
Former Republic of Ireland and Liverpool player, Ray Houghton

'The only thing I have in common with George Best is that we come from the same place, play for the same club and were discovered by the same man.'
Norman Whiteside, former Manchester United and Northern Ireland player

'The thing that sticks in my mind is that he always made time for anyone who came up to him – and that was a steady stream from the moment he got there. He asked for our names the first time he came in and he never forgot them ... He would always treat us with respect and involve us in conversations which made an otherwise boring shift highly enjoyable. I feel proud to have known him even if it was only for a short time. He was always genuine and fun to be around.'

Meg Williams worked in a bar George used to frequent

'I can remember him smiling at me that night and it was so infectious you wanted to smile with him. For me it was an absolute pleasure and he was an absolute gentleman.'

Dave Davis, member of the public, about meeting Best in 2003

'He was so generous, so warm and he must have been going through hell (he had just broken up with Miss World). He told a few jokes, shook us all by the hand and left. We were all stunned. We don't expect anybody of that stature to do that. We all followed his exploits on and off the field. But he had no ego, no conceit. He was just a lovely bloke, one of the boys. A real superstar.'

John Young, member of the public, about meeting Best

'At football grounds in Britain last weekend, players and spectators stood in silence in memory of George Best, a ceremony once reserved to honour the war dead. Mr Best last played top-class football more than 30 years ago, when most of today's spectators would have been too young to see him play. However, if anyone doubted his divinity, they were reassured by veteran reporters whose memories of him have remained impressively vivid. 'I can still see him now,' wrote one, 'slim, boyish, dark hair shining in the floodlights as he scythed though the defence ... It was sheer poetry. I can remember leaping to my feet against all the etiquette of the press box, so stunning was the fluid scoring movement.'

It is unlikely the rituals for George Best will be repeated. But academics researching the social history of Britain in the second half of the twentieth century may perhaps grant him the immortality of a footnote.'

Extract from Economist *obituary*

'He threw everything away through the drink. He owned a bar called Hard Times and he was never out of there. There is maybe only Pelé who was better than him and I would definitely put him in the top ten footballers of all time. But I'd also put him in the top ten idiots of all time too.'

Tommy Smith, Liverpool contemporary

'The difference between today's soccer heroes and Best is not just that he remains peerless as a footballer. Best was – and will remain – loved. Best was loved in a way today's players will never be. Best had the gift of bringing out people's better nature. It is no mean feat to lie on your deathbed with the love and thoughts of thousands of people – as the Beatles sang way back then – across the universe.'
Keith Duggan

'He has left us a million memories, all of them good ones. What I remember was his courage.'
Sir Alex Ferguson, Manchester United manager

'Thanks for the memories. You were the Mozart of football.'
Elton John

BEST MOMENTS

Remembering and visualising some of the best Best moments can be a wonderful trip down memory-lane. Here are some favourites in no particular order.

There is an incredible video compilation at http://www.pdqwebhosting.com/george.htm to help you! It would almost bring you to tears. Enjoy!

1. Eddie McCready was tenaciously dispossessed by Best who lobbed the goalkeeper from the edge of the area. Manchester United v. Chelsea 1965.

2. Best rounded the Benfica keeper in the European Cup quarter-final, 1966.

3. In the same game, the European Cup quarter-final, 1966, at Benfica, Best glided past the defence to score his second on twelve minutes. Although he

scored only two goals that night he is remembered for his 'hat-trick' when sporting a sombrero at the airport on his return from Portugal. Classic Best.

4. His best display for Northern Ireland was in the 1-0 win over Scotland, Windsor Park, 1967. 'I just felt the buzz that day, felt ... I could try almost anything and expect to get away with it ... every time I got the ball, I ran straight at their defence.'

5. Best scored six goals against Northampton Town in the 1970 FA Cup.

6. Best dribbled from half-way and evaded a Ron 'Chopper' Harris 'tackle' in the 1970 League Cup fourth round at Old Trafford against Chelsea. Harris recounted how the following season this goal was on the start of 'Match of the Day' – '... and every time I saw it I'd still think I'd got him'.

7. Best turned Manchester United team-mate Nobby Styles inside out as he scored when Northern Ireland beat England 1-0, 1970.

8. Best lobbed Pat Jennings, his international colleague, in the Manchester United game against Tottenham Hotspur in 1971.

9. Best performed a classic double shuffle against Southampton 1971 (Manchester United were wearing yellow shirts).

10. The classic disallowed goal was when Best nicked the ball from the English goalkeeper Gordon Banks as he went to kick the ball out. The ball looped over Banks' head and Best headed into an empty net. Northern Ireland against England, 1971.

11. Best was driven wide but still scored the winner off the far post. Manchester United v. Sheffield United 1971.

12. There was 'Harlem Globetrotters' type foolery with Rodney Marsh when they tackled each other at Fulham against Hereford United, 1976.

13. Best scored a wonder goal for San José Earthquakes against Fort Lauderdale Strikers in 1981. 'Unbelievable, the cheek, the arrogance, the sheer genius of this man leaving the defence collapsed in a pile around his feet', said the commentator. Best later said about the goal that 'It gave me a lot of pleasure'.

14. 'Mr Best, where did it all go wrong?' said a Belfast night porter at a Birmingham hotel, after getting a £50 tip, while surveying the Dom Perignon, the current Miss World in a negligée and £20,000 in gambling winnings scattered on the bed.

CHRONOLOGY

1946
22 May: Born George Best, in Belfast.

1961: Joins Manchester United as an amateur, aged fifteen. Travels from Belfast to Old Trafford with Eric McMordie, who went on to play for Middlesbrough. The pair return to Northern Ireland because they are homesick. Best goes back to Manchester on his own. Is placed with the Manchester Ship Canal company as a tea-boy.

1963
22 May : Signs professional forms for Manchester United.
14 September: Makes First Division debut against West Bromwich Albion at Old Trafford. Manchester United win 1-0.
28 December: Scores first league goal v Burnley at Old Trafford.

1964

15 April: Makes Northern Ireland debut in 3-2 win against Wales in Swansea.

14 November: Scores first goal for Northern Ireland in a 1-2 away defeat against Switzerland.

1965: Helps Manchester United win their first league championship in eight years. Scores ten goals in 41 league appearances.

1966

9 March: Scores twice in the opening ten minutes as Manchester United beat Benfica 5-1 in the European Cup quarter final tie in Portugal. Best is hailed as 'El Beatle' by the Portuguese newspaper *Bola*.

1967: Manchester United win the league championship. Best scores ten goals in 42 league games.

1968

4 May: English Footballer of the Year Award.

29 May: Manchester United become the first English team to win the European Cup, Best scoring in a 4-1 extra-time triumph over Benfica at Wembley.

16 October: Sent off for the first time in his playing career against Spanish team Estudiantes at Old Trafford.

December: Awarded European Footballer of the Year.

1970

7 February: Scores six goals in Manchester United's 8-2 win against Northampton Town (away) in the fifth round of the FA Cup. It is Best's first game after suspension for knocking the ball out of the referee's hands after the League Cup tie against Manchester City.

18 April: Sent off playing for Northern Ireland against Scotland after spitting and throwing mud at the referee.

1971

8 January: Misses the train taking the Manchester United team to play Chelsea in London. Best spends the weekend with actress Sinéad Cusack. The story makes the front and back pages of the national newspapers.

21 April: Scores his only hat trick for Northern Ireland in a 5-0 win against Cyprus in Belfast.

13 October: Refused permission by Manchester United to play for Northern Ireland against USSR in Belfast after he receives death threats.

23 October: Best receives further death threats that he will be shot while playing for Manchester United in an away game at Newcastle United. Best plays and scores the only goal of the game. Security is tight and Best receives police protection after the match.

17 November: Best is the subject of television's 'This Is Your Life'.

1972

8 January: Dropped for the home game against Wolverhampton Wanderers after missing training. Best flies to London and spends the weekend with the then Miss Great Britain, Carolyn Moore.

10 January: Best returns to Old Trafford and is fined two week's wages (about £400). He is instructed to do extra training and ordered to move from his home to his previous digs with Mrs Mary Fullaway.

20 May: Best is in Marbella when he announces that he has decided to retire from football.

7 July: Best flies back to Britain and announces that he will again play for Manchester United. The club suspends him for two weeks for a breach of contract and the Marbella affair and order Best into lodgings with Pat Crerand and his family. Best's house is put up for sale and he moves back into digs with Mrs Mary Fullaway.

19 December: O'Farrell is sacked by Manchester United. Best sends a letter to the club directors to say that he is finished with football. This is the second time he announces his retirement.

1973

19 June : Best declares that he will not play football again.

27 August: Manchester United chairman Louis Edwards states that the club would like Best to start training again.

28 August: Best announces that, after talks with Manchester United manager Tommy Docherty, that he would like to give football another try.

November: Opens nightclub 'Slack Alice' in Manchester.

1974

1 January: Best plays in his last game for Manchester United in the fixture away at Queen's Park Rangers. His team loses 0-3.

5 January: Omitted from the Manchester United team to play Plymouth Argyle in the FA Cup third Round tie at Old Trafford. Best walks out of the ground vowing never to play for the club again. Plays for Jewish Guild of Johannesburg, but his short spell in South Africa is characterised by his heavy drinking and gambling lifestyle.

5 August: Plays for Dunstable Town in a friendly fixture against Manchester United Reserves.

1975

Plays for Stockport County on loan, making three league appearances and scoring two goals.

28 December: Plays in the first of three League of Ireland games for Cork Celtic.

1976

19 January: Best is sacked by Cork Celtic because of his 'lack of enthusiasm'.

20 February: Arrives in Los Angeles.

17 April: Makes his debut for Los Angeles Aztecs in a 1-2 away defeat against San José Earthquakes.

4 September: Makes his league debut for F u l h a m (47 appearances, ten goals) in the home fixture against Bristol Rovers. Best scores after 71 seconds in front of a 21,127 crowd.

13 October: Makes 'comeback' appearance for Northern Ireland in an away fixture against Holland almost three years after his last international game.

1977

12 November: Plays his final game for Fulham in the 0-2 away defeat at Stoke City.

1978

24 January: Marries Angela MacDonald James, aged 25, in Las Vegas.

June: Transferred to Fort Lauderdale Strikers.

12 October: Best's mother, Ann, dies aged 54 after her own battle with alcoholism.

1979

October: Manchester United refuses Best a testimonial match.

16 November: Best signs for Hibernian from Fulham.

24 November: Makes his Hibernian debut in the away match at St Mirren. Best scores, though his new team lose 1-2; 13,670 spectators attend the game.

1980

11 October: Plays in his final game for Hibernian in a home match against Falkirk.

1981

6 February: Son, Calum Milan Best, is born in San José.

26 September: Manchester United considers re-signing Best.

11 December: Middlesborough prematurely announce that a deal has been done to sign Best.

1982

November: Best is declared bankrupt.

1983

26 March: Best makes his debut for AFC Bournemouth in the home game against Newport County, watched by a crowd of 9,121 spectators. Plays five times for Bournemouth before finally retiring.

7 May: Best makes his final league appearance in England for AFC Bournemouth in the home game against Wigan Athletic, fifteen days short of his thirty-seventh birthday.

3 July: Best plays in the first of four league games for struggling Brisbane Lions in Australia.

1984

28 January: Plays for Tobermore United in an Irish

Cup match at home to Ballymena United.

3 November: Best is charged and then bailed for a drink-driving offence. He later fails to turn up at court, is subsequently arrested and assaults a policeman.

3 December: Receives a three-month prison sentence for drink-driving and the assault on a policeman. He is bailed pending an appeal.

17 December: Best's appeal is dismissed and he is sent to Pentonville Prison, though ten days later he is transferred to Ford open prison in Sussex.

1985

8 February: Released from prison after serving eight weeks of a twelve-week sentence.

1986

Divroced from his wife Angela MacDonald James.

1987

December: The Irish Football Association refuses to grant Best a testimonial game.

1988

8 August: Best has his own testimonial match at Windsor Park, Belfast. Approximately 25,000 spectators watch the game. Best scores a sublime chip from 30 yards. Raises £75,000 to help stave off bankruptcy.

1990
19 September: Appears on the Terry Wogan Show.

1992
5 May: Receives bankruptcy discharge.

1995
24 July: Marries for a second time to Alexandra Jane Macadam Pursey, aged 23, at Chelsea Town Hall, London.

1996
22 May: BBC2 devotes an entire evening's viewing to celebrate Best's fiftieth birthday.

1998: joins Sky Sports as a football pundit.

1999
26 May: Best leaves the European Champions' League final four minutes early and misses Manchester United's two late dramatic goals which seal a 2-1 victory for his old team against Bayern Munich.

2000
23 January: Best honoured by the Football Writers' Association with a unique Services to Football award.
March: Admitted to hospital.

2001

20 May: Named the top Manchester footballer of the past 50 years by a *Manchester Evening News* Sunday Pink Panel.

17 September: Best's autobiography *Blessed* is published by Ebury Press.

December: Reveals he is on standby for a liver transplant.

13 December: Best presented with an honorary degree from Queen's University, Belfast.

2002

3 April: Awarded the freedom of Castlereagh, the area of east Belfast where he grew up.

30 July: Goes into hospital for a liver transplant.

8 December: Awarded a Lifetime Achievement Award at the BBC Sports Personality of the Year.

2003

August: Announces he is selling his trophies, including his 1968 European Footballer of the Year award, to raise money to buy a home in Greece.

2004

February: Banned from driving for twenty months after pleading guilty to drink-driving.

April: Divorced from wife Alex.

2005

July: Cleared over allegations of indecently assaulting a teenage girl.

3 October: Doctors at the private Cromwell Hospital in west London reveal that Best is in intensive care with kidney problems.

28 October: Best remains in hospital and, while there is a slight improvement in his condition, he remains in a serious condition. Best allows the British newspaper *The News of the World* to print a photograph of him in hospital, as a warning about the dangers of alcohol. In the photograph, Best looks gaunt and his skin has a yellow pallor due to his malfunctioning liver. Tubes are attached to his bruised body. Best's agent Phil Hughes, commenting on the photograph, said: 'George could never beat his drink problem, but he told me, "I hope my plight can act as a warning to others".'

23 November: Best deteriorated and was back on a ventilator.

25 November: Best dies aged 59.

3 December: Funeral in Belfast attended by 100,000 mourners.

CAREER STATISTICS

Pre -1963 Cregagh Boys' Club

1963-1974 Manchester United: 466 games, 178 goals, (League 361/137, FA Cup 46/21, League Cup 25/9, Europe 34/11)

1974 Jewish Guild of Johannesburg: 5 games

1975 Dunstable Town (friendlies)

1975 Stockport County: 3 games, 2 goals

1976 Cork Celtic: 3 games, 0 goals

1976 Los Angeles Aztecs: 24 games, 15 goals

1976-1977 Fulham: 47 games, 10 goals

1977-1978 Los Angeles Aztecs: 37 games, 14 goals

1978-1979 Fort Lauderdale Strikers: 33 games, 7 goals

1979-1980 Hibernian: 22 games, 3 goals

1980-1981 San Jose Earthquakes: 56 games, 21 goals

1983 Bournemouth: 5 games, 0 goals

1983 Brisbane Lions: 4 games, 0 goals

1984 Tobermore United: 1 game, 0 goals

(Tobermore United is a Northern Ireland football club)

International: 1964-1978 - Northern Ireland: 37 games, 9 goals

HONOURS

Football League Championship winners medal, 1965 and 1967

UEFA European Cup winners medal, 1968

European Footballer of the Year, 1968

Football Writers' Association Footballer of the Year, 1968

Holds the record for the most goals by a Manchester United player in a single match, six against Northampton Town, FA Cup fifth round on 8 February 1970.

2000 Honoured by the Football Writers' Association

2001 Named the top Manchester footballer of the past 50 years by a *Manchester Evening News* Sunday Pink Panel.

2002 Awarded a Lifetime Achievement Award at the BBC Sports Personality of the Year ceremony.

Freeman of Castlereagh, 2002

Honorary Doctorate of Queen's University, Belfast, 2001

Career Statistics

MANCHESTER UNITED MANAGERS

Alex Ferguson	Nov 1986 to present
Ron Atkinson	Jun 1981 to Nov 1986
Dave Sexton	Jul 1977 to Apr 1981
Tommy Docherty	Dec 1972 to Jul 1977
Frank O'Farrell	Jun 1971 to Dec 1972
Matt Busby	Dec 1970 to Jun 1971
Wilfred McGuinness	Jun 1969 to Dec 1970
Matt Busby	Aug 1958 to Jun 1969
Jimmy Murphy (Caretaker)	Feb 1958 to Aug 1958
Matt Busby	Feb 1945 to Feb 1958

SELECTED MANCHESTER UNITED TEAM SHEETS
It is interesting to note the changes in team lineout and league success over the Manchester United career of George Best:

Manchester United 1: West Bromich Albion 0
14 September 1963 at Old Trafford
Manager: Sir Matt Busby
Best's first game for Manchester United
Gregg, Dunne A., Cantwell, Crerand, Foulkes, Setters, Best, Stiles, Sadler D., Chisnall, Charlton
[Champions Everton 61 points, Manchester United nineteenth, 34 points]

Manchester United 4: Benfica 1
29 May 1968 European Cup Final at Wembley.
Manager: Sir Matt Busby
Stepney, Brennan, Dunne A., Crerand, Foulkes, Stiles, Best, Kidd, Charlton, Sadler D., Aston J. Jr

[Champions Manchester City 58 points, Manchester United second, 56 points]

Manchester City 3: Manchester United 4
5 May 1971 Maine Road
Manager: Sir Matt Busby
Best's last game under Sir Matt
Stepney, O'Neill, Burns, Crerand, James, Sadler D., Law D., Gowling, Charlton, Kidd, Best.
[Champions Arsenal 65 points, Manchester United eighth, 43 points]

Manchester United 2: Southampton 1
25 November 1972 at Old Trafford
Manager: Frank O'Farrell
Best's last game under O'Farrell
Stepney, O'Neill, Dunne A., Morgan W., Edwards P., Buchan M., Best, MacDougall, Charlton, Davies W., Storey-Moore
[Champions Derby County 58 points, Manchester United 28th, 48 points]

Queens Park Rangers 3: Manchester United 0
1 January 1974 at Loftus Road.
Manager: Tommy Docherty
Best's last game for Manchester United
Stepney, Young, T., Houston, Greenhoff B., Holton, Buchan M., Morgan W., Macari, McIlroy, Graham. Best.
[Champions Leeds United 62 points, Manchester United twenty-first, 32 points, relegated]

References

Internet Site Sources and Fanzines
http://www.compusmart.ab.ca/icorry/BESTPage.htm
There is an absolutely brilliant video on this web page.
Clearly the definitive George Best web site.

Thanks to the following, whose newspaper and magazine articles have been used as sources: Ronald Atkin, Ross Benson, Peter Byrne, Tony Cascarino, Hunter Davies, Barry Davis, Keith Duggan, Eamon Holmes, James Lawton, Joe Lovejoy, Ivan Martin, Eamonn McCann, Roisin McCauley, Hugh McIlvanney, James Nesbit, Graham Nickless, Michael Parkinson, John Roberts, Les Scott, Euan Stretch, Mike Summerbee.

Best, Alex, *Always Alex: My Story,* Blake Publishing, 2005
Best, Angie, and, Nicola Pittam, *George and Me: My Autobiography*, Virgein Books, 2002
Best, George, *Best of Both Worlds*, Pelham Books, 1968
Best, George with Grahame Wright, *Where do I Go From*

Here? McDonald Queen Anne, 1982

Best, George with Ross Benson, *The Good, The Bad and the Bubbly*, Simon and Schuster Ltd.

Best, George with Les Scott, *The Best of Times. My Favourite Football Stories.* Simon and Schuster UK Ltd. 1994

George Best with Roy Collins, *Blessed.* Ebury Press, London. 2001

George Best, Scoring at Half-Time, Ebury Press, London. 2003

Lovejoy, Joe, *Bestie: A Portrait of a Legend*, Pan. 1999

Martin, Ivan, *George Best The Legend in Pictures*, Appletree Press, 2006

Meek, David, *George Best: Tribute to a Legend*, Weidenfeld & Nicolson, 2005

Parkinson, Michael, *Best An Intimate Biography*, Hutchinson & Co (Publishers) Ltd. 1975